Stewards of Creation

Living as Christians in an age of environmental crisis

by

Dr Tobias Thornes

WASH HOUSE PUBLISHING

Non-fiction

Published by Wash House Publishing 2024

Printed on demand by CPI Group.
The CPI Group is committed to the prevention of pollution and continual improvement to reduce our effect on the environment.

Copyright © Tobias Thornes, 2024.

ISBN 978-1-7391357-3-7

All Rights Reserved. All or part of this publication may be reproduced, reprinted or otherwise disseminated only when accompanied by acknowledgement of the author.

About the Author

Dr Tobias Thornes is a Christian, scientist and writer. He studied Physics & Astronomy at the University of Durham, before obtaining a DPhil in Atmospheric Physics at the University of Oxford. He is at the time of writing in training for ministry in the Church of England. He has written numerous articles, papers and books on topics ranging from physics and environmental science to poetry and economics. His recent publications include:

The Problem with Money: Towards a New Economics (2018)
The Problem with Money: Solving the Problem (2019)
Requiem for the Intercity 125: Poems of Travel and Change (2019)
Growing into God (2020)
The Psalter: in Rhyming Verse (2021)
The Bible: in Rhyming Verse (2022)
Singapore to London by Rail (2022)

To His Majesty King Charles III,
an inspiration of Christian compassion for our world.

And all Israel heard of the judgment which the king had judged; and they feared the king: for they saw that the wisdom of God was in him, to do judgment.
1 Kings 3:28

Contents

Foreword	6
1: Why are we Here?	11
2: The Life is More than Meat	23
3: The Body is More than Raiment	37
4: The House on the Rock	48
5: Lambs among Wolves	60
6: Blessed are the Poor	71
7: Discerning the Time	81

Foreword

> Be ye not as your fathers, unto whom the former prophets have cried, saying 'Turn ye now from your evil ways, and from your evil doings,' but they did not hear, nor hearken unto me, saith the Lord. (Zechariah 1:4)

> Turn ye unto me, saith the Lord of hosts, and I will turn unto you. (Zechariah 1:3)

Christians today are living in unprecedented times. Our forebears have sinned; we have sinned, in the way we have lived our lives and despoiled our planet. The many crises we face are the result of our failure to steward the Earth – from climate change and its associated floods, droughts, and storms, to the extinction of entire species, and the misery of millions of people living in exploitation around the world. We have failed to listen to the modern-day prophets who have warned us of the consequences of our actions.

Yet this is far from the first time that humans have failed to follow God's commands, ignoring His prophets, and have acted selfishly instead. From the story of Adam & Eve right at the start in Genesis 3, the Bible records the long history of mankind's turbulent relationship with our Creator, sometimes worshipping and humbly obeying Him, and yet always turning away again when temptations arise. But whilst we might keep giving up on God, the Bible assures us that He never gives up on us. The prophet Zechariah, speaking to God's chosen people of Israel two and a half millennia ago, sends not a message of despair, but one of hope. They had sinned; their fathers had sinned, and failed to keep God's law, worshipping other gods and acting with cruelty towards one another. Yet, Zechariah tells us, it is never too late to turn back to God.

Climate change, the defining issue of our age, is a symptom of a wider disconnection of modern-day humanity from the natural world around us. We have lost our loving relationship with the natural world, and exploited it far beyond its ability to sustainably provide resources to everyone, acting out of greed rather than need. Only now, after decades of over-consumption by the wealthy minority, is this coming back to haunt us. But we should not, as Christians, despair: we know that God created all this, the splendour of the Earth and of the universe as a whole. We know also that He will not abandon us, but will help us to undo the damage that has been done and restore balance in the natural world: if only we are willing to humbly listen and act in accordance with His will.

Unfortunately the Church has been, and continues to be, too slow in responding to the environmental crisis and converting our prayers for plenty for everyone into actions that might make this a reality. This book aims to help us to do just this. Although the implications are applicable to all humanity, here we take a distinctly Christian viewpoint, beginning with a brief review of why, according to the

Foreword

Bible, we are here on this Earth in the first place. We shall see that inherent within our creation as human beings is a duty and expectation to lovingly steward the world. In chapters 2-6, we shall see how this duty can be converted from an abstract love into real, concrete actions that we can all carry out in our individual churches and our individual lives. We shall look at all the basics: food, drink, buildings, travel, possessions, and see how the ordinary decisions we make with regard to each of these can have profound consequences for other people and the wellbeing of our living planet as a whole. It is therefore required of each of us to make those decisions lovingly and carefully.

Of course, none of us can change the world by ourselves. It may seem that to make small sacrifices in our own lives is fruitless when there are so many other people in world causing damage to the environment. But as Christians we know that there are two reasons why this is not the case. First, as Jesus Himself showed us, the fact that we cannot make a difference to everyone all at once should not stop us from making a difference in our own immediate environment. He was always willing to stop and speak and listen and heal – curing those around Him of their diseases, even if those diseases continued to be rife elsewhere. If we can improve our own local environment through avoiding polluting means of transport, or the wellbeing of a few animals through the decisions we make about what to eat, it is our Christian duty to do so.

Secondly, as people of faith we know that God hears the prayers we speak and sees the actions we perform. Just as He was placated by sacrifice in the Old Testament, and Himself made the ultimate sacrifice for us in the New, we know that the small sacrifices we make in our own lives can be prayers to Him that will invoke His mercy and help. It's not that God wouldn't love us if we didn't make sacrifices. But if it's our actions that are the problem – our choices leading to the destruction of the environment – it's no good praying to Him for help in words if we won't change our deeds accordingly. If we make only little sacrifices, in our own lives, that we know contribute a drop in the ocean to what's required for a better, greener, fairer world, God will see these sacrifices and will magnify our efforts to do so much more than we are able to achieve on our own strength. Our faith as Christians therefore gives us a particular incentive to act.

This book is rooted in scripture, and especially in Jesus' own example and teachings. Most of the chapters begin with a Biblical quotation, often from the Gospel of Luke, before applying this teaching to the context of our contemporary environmental crisis. All quotations are from the King James Version, a translation that, as well as poetically and attractively expressing the scriptures in English, remains especially faithful to the original Greek. This is an intentionally small book, not weighed down by copious examples or citations, as it is intended to be read quickly and easily, but throughout its seven chapters it will become plain that, far from having very little to say on environmental issues, the Bible is replete with teachings that are very applicable to this important but too often neglected topic.

Foreword

I do not wish to argue here that everyone should be able to change every aspect of their lives in response to the environmental crisis, still less to cause anyone to feel guilty for the contribution that every one of us makes towards it. It's a problem that we all face, together, brought about by a way of living that we did not choose but have unintentionally become part of. What is most important is that we recognise this – recognise that we all have a part to play, and that we can come to a solution, by working together. One of the wonderful things about being part of the Christian Church is the realisation that we are never alone.

My hope is that you will read this book not as an indictment but as an invitation – an invitation to the whole Church to transform the way we live in accordance with our calling to steward the world and love one another. We have for too long been caught up in a consumerist culture that has led us to be complicit in so much harm to our environment and the world's poor. Now is the time to challenge this culture, and to lead the way towards a better future, buoyed up, inspired and directed by the Christian virtues of faith, love and humility. The world looks to religion for answers on moral issues, and we must not fail to show the way and to exercise the compassion for creation that is God's will. This may not always be easy, but it will always be right.

Tobias Thornes
Hadzor
August 2024

1

Why are we Here?

The Bible gives us two reasons for the creation of mankind. The first, most explicit reason is given right at the start, in Genesis, chapter 1, verse 28. Having created mankind, God tells them to 'be fruitful, and multiply, and replenish the Earth and subdue it: and have dominion over the fish of the sea, and over the fowl of the air, and over every living thing that moveth upon the Earth.' Thus, according to Genesis, the purpose of God creating human beings 'in His own image' was that they should produce more human beings, and spread through the whole Earth to replenish and subdue it, having 'dominion' over it.

The command 'replenish' implies responsibility – mankind is responsible for carrying on the work that God has done in creating the Earth, by using their own god-like creative powers to continually replenish the world He has made. The command to 'subdue' implies power: humans are to bring the world under their control. And the concept of 'dominion' involves both of these things: mankind is to have control over creation, all the living beings that God has made, but this power is to be used to the benefit of the Earth that they are given to rule over.

The word we might best use to describe such a commission as this is that of 'stewardship'. A steward has responsibility, and a steward has power, but only insofar as the steward has been appointed this power by a higher authority: a steward is a caretaker, not a king.

The second purpose that we are given in the Bible as human beings is linked to another key word used in Genesis 1:28, 'fruitful'. Taken alone in this passage, 'fruitful' doesn't necessarily imply anything more than simply 'abundant in the fruit of the womb' – in a literal sense, it relates to humankind 'multiplying' in the Earth by having children. But the rest of the Bible – remember that we are here still on page 1 – fills in a bit more detail about what being 'fruitful' in a broader sense actually entails. First, the people God chose to be His own, the children of Israel, were instructed to keep His commandments, so that, as we are told in Exodus 19:5, 'you shall be a peculiar treasure unto me above all people: for all the Earth is mine'. In other words, God values as treasure those who are fruitful in doing as He commands. The fruits He harvests from them are their good deeds.

For Christians, Jesus Christ extended God's covenant – the agreement made perpetually with the children of Israel, the Jews – to the whole world. In the Gospels, Jesus too uses the metaphors of fruitfulness and of treasure when He speaks to us about what God requires of mankind if they are to be adopted as God's children. According to Jesus, what God wants of us is not our ritual sacrifice, but relationship – that is why we each were brought into existence in the first place – and the fruits exhibited by a deep, nourishing relationship are love, faithfulness and joy. Our purpose in life, then, is to experience and cause others to experience true joy, true faithfulness and true love. Such virtues characterise a healthy and fruitful relationship with God.

Hence, we see that Biblically there are two purposes to our existence as human beings: to steward the Earth, and to enjoy loving relationships. That is why God made us, and this truth ought really to be borne in mind throughout all that we do in the course of our entire lives. After all, to do anything contrary to this our purpose in life is pointless, and to be motivated by any incentive that is opposed to what God purposes for us is sinful: it is harmful to ourselves as much as it is to anybody else, since it undermines our very essence and the meaning of our lives. Life devoid of lasting meaning is miserable indeed. Furthermore, what God is expecting of us is not difficult, in that when He created us He made us fit for purpose. He equipped us with all that we need to fulfil His purposes for us, and He does not demand from any of us more than He has given us the capacity to do.

God has equipped us all with the ability to love and to feel love, and His greatest and only true commandment to us in Christ simply requires us to utilise this ability. As we read in Matthew 23:37, 'thou shalt love the Lord thy God with all thy heart, and with all thy soul, and with all thy mind.' This is the first commandment. Jesus goes on to give a second, 'Thou shalt love thy neighbour as thyself.' He explains, 'for on these two commandments hang all the law and the prophets.' The entire Old Testament law – which runs to hundreds of commandments – was all fundamentally about these two commandments, which are at the heart of our purpose in life as human beings.

Likewise, in the Gospel of John, chapter 15, Jesus intimates that 'herein is my Father glorified, that ye bear much fruit; so shall ye be my disciples. As the Father hath loved me, so have I loved you: continue ye in my love. If ye keep my commandments, ye shall abide in my love.' And what is Jesus' commandment? 'This is my commandment, that ye love one another, as I have loved you.' To love one another as Jesus loved us, as humans, is indeed to exhibit a deep, unconditional and unbounded love: for Jesus loved us so much, Christians believe, that He was willing to lay down His own life, His whole life, for the sake of all humanity when He allowed Himself to be crucified. To His enemies and critics, this looked like the ultimate disgrace, the throwing away of His life to die the fruitless death of a criminal. But what is true fruitfulness? To have such a love as this – a self-sacrificial love – is true fruitfulness, and is in fact to fulfil our purpose here in Earth. There could be no better act for Him to perform.

Simple as our purpose may be, and suited as we are to perform it – because we are made in God's image as Genesis 1 tells us – it is not always easy in this life to live up to this purpose. The whole story of humanity's development from the dawn of civilisation right down to the present attests to this fact. Time and again, humankind has shown itself to be incapable of self-sacrificial, unconditional love for one another or for God, and to be corrupt, self-serving and utterly untrustworthy when it comes to the stewardship of creation. Since we first fell out of friendship with God and decided to do things our own way – a fall from grace that the Genesis story of the Garden of Eden describes – the temptation to treat the self as God and to act out of self-interest has blighted humanity. Reliant on our own inventions and hoarding up our own produce and possessions, we act in a way wholly opposed to what our true purpose in life is and has always been.

We, who uniquely amongst all God's creations have been given the capacity to be selfish or to be selfless – to live our lives for our own material gain or to live for others and for God – have time and again chosen the former attitude to life, to the detriment of one another and indeed of the whole Earth. The moment of our first disgrace is described biblically in the story of Adam and Eve's 'fall' in Genesis 3, and modern science pinpoints mankind's decline in fortunes to around that the time that we developed a sedentary, farming lifestyle around 10,000 BC. It was at this point that life became much harder, because we had to farm rather than to forage, with a larger population to feed. Society became more stratified as a few began to accumulate wealth and power whilst the majority remained poor, because for the first time we had the capacity to gather and store for ourselves private material possessions much more numerous than those that one could easily carry around. Money was invented to facilitate this new inequality.

It was at that same time that humanity, besotted with the new-found technology of farming, began to shape the world that God had created to suit our own ends, not His. Large mammals – 'megafauna' – were

Why are we Here?

hunted to extinction from Europe to Australasia as humans sought to protect their own flocks and herds from predation. Forests started to be cleared to make way for farms, and fields to be planted up with crops that we wanted to eat. Climate change, too, of the anthropogenic (man-made) kind began then, as patterns of rainfall altered in response to the changed layout of the landscape. It is thought that the Sahara – once a relatively green and flourishing land – turned into desert partly as a result of humanity's changes. Certainly, the deforestation of large areas of land, such as the British Isles, represented a stark change to local environments, to the detriment of other species that were living there and to the benefit only of humanity. Think of a thick forest resounding with birdsong, as Britain once was, and look at Spaghetti Junction today, and it becomes obvious that humanity has destroyed at least part of the splendour of God's creation and traded it for something infinitely less beautiful.

Such major alterations made in the interests of man might be considered to be a dereliction of our duty as stewards, representing the fallen nature of humanity as seen through Christian eyes. On the other hand, one could argue that changing our environment was necessary for the collective wellbeing of a human population that had exceeded the numbers that could be sustained by hunter-gathering, and required there to be settled, farming communities for it to continue to grow. God had given us responsibility, yes, for looking after His creation, but He had also commanded us to multiply, and had intended for us to use Earth's resources to that end. At least the changes made to our planet by our ancient predecessors were, with the exception of the extinction of some large animal species, largely reversible. Indeed, up until fairly recently on the timescale of human activities, the Earth's biosphere seems to have been flourishing despite our settlements and activities.

Two hundred and fifty years ago, Earth was home to around six million different species of plants and animals, very few of which were on the brink of extinction. Most human societies lived by what we would now call 'sustainable' means, working in harmony with nature and allowing the resources they depended upon to be replenished. Humanity was far from perfect, but it was still in large part fulfilling its purposes and responsibilities in stewarding creation as decreed by God.

The current suite of changes being made to our planet is something quite different. Climate change, biodiversity loss and the destruction of the natural world represent an unprecedented threat to all living creatures, brought about in the space of only 250 years since the beginning of the Industrial Revolution. These changes leave no corner of the world untouched, and are all brought about – and currently accelerating – as a result of human actions. This time, they are not reversible except on a timescale of many thousands of years, and therefore have the power to affect – or even extinguish – countless future generations of both human beings and other animals.

Why are we Here?

The greatest indicator of just how much things have gone wrong is the fact that at least 1 in 8 of all the world's species are at the immanent risk of extinction – indeed, the Earth faces the sixth 'mass extinction event' of all history. Previous such events were caused by asteroid impacts and super-volcanoes. This one is being caused by a component of life itself: the very species entrusted with looking after the Earth and its inhabitants, humanity.

Could there be any greater indictment against us? Could there be any more flagrant a dereliction of our duty, or more heinous insult to the God who created us? We are destroying His handiwork; we are not stewarding His planet but pillaging it for ourselves; this is not dominion but domination. Nor can we any longer claim that what we do is done out of necessity, in a world where one third of the human beings live in luxury and are the root cause of nearly all the destruction, whilst two thirds live in relative poverty and feel the brunt of climate change's effects. We have not only failed to share with other species, we have failed to share with one another. There should be enough for everyone, if we all lived simply and reverently. But those who are the best-off are taking far too much, and it is clear whom God will hold responsible for the mess that mankind has made.

In Matthew 21, Jesus tells the parable of the vineyard. He tells it to critique the leaders of the Jews, who had been entrusted with the fruit of the vineyard – the Jewish people – and yet exploited it for themselves instead, abusing their position of responsibility. But those leaders were to be stewards of God's people, just as humanity as a whole are stewards of God's Earth. In the parable, when the owner of the vineyard sends servants to collect the fruit, the stewards beat them up and even kill some of them, including the owner's own son. These servants represent the martyred prophets God sent to Israel only for them to be killed by crooked kings, with Jesus Himself, the Son of God, represented by the son who was slain.

The parallels with humanity's situation now are plain. The 'prophets' who speak up against the destruction of nature, and the pollution and exploitation of the Earth, are ignored; people die from climate change as a result of the powers of this world refusing to take proper action because they don't want to risk their own wealth and status. At the end of the parable, Jesus asks 'what will the owner of the vineyard do to those husbandmen?' Dare we ask the question of what God will do to those who exploit and destroy the natural world to feed their own greed today?

The husbandmen were not set over the vineyard to steal its fruits, but to look after it. They undermined their own purpose in stealing for themselves, and the result was that they ultimately lost everything, having caused so much death and injury in the process of trying to keep it. We too undermine our own purpose in life and risk losing everything if we destroy God's world for the sake of our own selfish, short-term gains.

What, then, are people of faith – God's Church – going to do about this? We may be called to be good stewards of creation, good husbandmen – but we live in

Why are we Here?

a society that has turned away from both God and the human duty of stewardship. A fixation on money, on material growth, on selfish gain and unnecessary material luxuries has driven a culture of consumerism and accelerated the destruction of our planet in recent decades. This can hardly be said to be the fault of the Church, when so many of the bad decisions have been made by big businesses and misguided governments over which Christians have little, if any, direct influence, in the context of an increasingly secularised society. That society is, it seems, eager to capitalise on the technological advances afforded by our ever-increasing understanding of scientific truth without simultaneously subjecting the use and abuse of that technology to rigorous moral scrutiny that we as theists believe only religion can provide. The result is a panoply of social and environmental crises, caused by the immoral application of well-intentioned industrial technologies. Such technologies are all too efficient at consuming Earth's resources rapidly, and converting them into cash for somebody at everybody's expense.

In light of this, the Church's role and power can seem to be insignificant. Yet nonetheless our calling remains, as Christians, to be good stewards of creation, and not to stand by and watch it be destroyed. We cannot in good conscience simply ignore the issue.

Concerning the Church's role in environmentalism, therefore, two salient points must be borne in mind. First, the Church is not entirely innocent of the crimes against nature being perpetrated by modern-day mankind. By its very failure to speak out vociferously on this issue for so long, with apparent indifference to the destruction of vast swathes of the natural world when set against other moral issues such as poverty and peace, the Church has been complicit in the environmental crisis. To paraphrase Jesus, we ought to have done this – spoken out and acted on our duty to look after the planet – and not to have left the other undone – campaigning on other important moral issues.

By going along with wider society's use of throwaway plastics, fossil fuels and industrially produced meat, for instance, the Church has joined in with mankind's rape of nature and has failed to take a stand for what we know to be morally right. We cannot justify such a position any longer: we must in our day to day lives and in our vocations as Christians, as well as in our church buildings and events, be true to our calling to care for creation in both word and deed.

Second, as people of faith we know that though our own actions may be small and seemingly inconsequential, it is the heart with which we act that is of most importance in God's eyes. Our God is certainly not small, and His will is the most consequential thing there ever could be. When God looks into our hearts, sees our acts of good will, and perceives the love in our everyday deeds of stewardship and compassion, He will hear our heartfelt prayers and magnify our efforts. For it is not by our own strength, but by His strength working through us, that we can do any good at all.

What we do in leading by example and speaking in protest against wrong can therefore have profound effects. Defending nature against the assault mankind

Why are we Here?

has set against it is a daunting, difficult, perhaps even impossible task for individuals or even a group of millions of individuals such as the Church to perform. But, says Jesus, 'the things that are impossible with men are possible with God.'

If we want God to forgive us our poor stewardship of His world, and to help us repair the damage that humanity has wrought, we must humbly come to Him in prayer, repent of the evils of humankind and act out that repentance in living sustainable lives. God will provide for the rest, give us what we need and equip us with faith, love and joy to last the journey.

After the resurrection, according to Luke's Gospel, Jesus asked His followers to 'preach to all nations repentance and forgiveness of sins.' That, then, is our task: by the way we live, the words we use and the actions we take, to show the world that the current way is wrong, but that things can be better. Repent of the evil, and God will restore all things to the goodness and harmony we were always meant to oversee as His stewards. This book is an attempt to show how this can be done, through the everyday choices that we make in our lives.

2

The Life is More than Meat

> Consider the ravens: for they neither sow nor reap, which have neither storehouse nor barn; and God feeds them. How much more are ye better than birds? (Luke 12:24)

In this well-known passage from Luke 12, Jesus tells us not to worry about food and drink because God provides us with all that we need.

It's not that food and drink are bad, to be despised or consumed regretfully as in some sort of penitential asceticism: far from it, for in His life Jesus Himself demonstrated the importance and enjoyment of food. Indeed, He criticises those who call Him a 'glutton and a drunkard', assuming that a prophet of God must conform to their own preconceptions of what he ought to be like, and expecting him to be fasting all the time. No, Jesus says, for 'your Father knows that you need these things.' And just as God provides for the birds of the air, so will He provide for us. We like to think of ourselves as much better than the birds – more cunning, more sophisticated, more worthy of what we gather up for ourselves. But Jesus, by contrast, teaches that we ought to be more like the other animals with which we share this world, and wrongly look down upon: we should be more humble, more simple, more trusting in

God to provide for us and more joyful and grateful for what we have. After all, most animals don't gather up food for themselves into a larder (squirrels perhaps excepted). God's creation provides for them – each species adapted to live in its own balanced ecosystem – and they joyfully receive and eat.

It is by refusing to humble ourselves to be more like the birds of God's garden that humanity has disrupted food webs, ecosystems and the ability to eat enough to survive on for species across the globe. True, Jesus wasn't talking about ecological catastrophe when He spoke about this in Luke 12, but what He was saying is that, although having enough to eat is essential for life, and to eat is good, food and drink is not what life's all about, and our own consumption of these things is not what we should be spending our lives thinking about. In Jesus' time, laws about what could and could not be eaten were prohibitive, and perhaps part of what He was saying was that people ought to get less hung-up about such matters, and concentrate on more important things in life, like loving each other. Yet His words also bear an important message for our own no-holes-barred culture of excessive consumption and desire for instant gratification. Jesus is calling on us to live more simply, to be less fussy, to be more grateful rather than gratified, and in doing so we shall also find that we live more sustainably.

Food comes up a lot in the Gospels, serving as an important metaphor for, often, things that Jesus claims are equally or even more important. The New Testament itself is sealed in bread and wine: the basic essentials of a meal at the time, and a clear indication that faith in this new covenant constitutes the bare essentials of a healthy life. The point Jesus seems to make, then, is that where many people place importance on food, fussing about how much they have and of what quality, we should instead place emphasis on what He gives us – the 'bread of life' to use St John's account – which is His very self, His example, His sacrifice, the truth that He shows us that life is really all about loving others, and thereby also loving God. Loving so much that we are willing to give our very lives for them.

Ordinary food is what keeps us alive, in this world at least. The 'bread of life' is what enables us to keep others alive, through compassion and the power of God's Spirit working through us. From this perspective, it is more natural and fruitful for us to be feeding each other, rather than seeking food for ourselves.

Jesus illustrates this when He sends out the seventy disciples, recounted in Luke 10: they are to go in pairs to preach the kingdom of God in the villages ahead of Him, 'and in the same house remain, eating and drinking such things as they give: for the labourer is worthy of his hire.' Jesus Himself ate with those who invited Him in, and made a point of feeding His disciples at the Last Supper, in Luke 22. When He'd visited Martha and Mary, in Luke 10, Martha was busy preparing things, but it was Mary whom Jesus praised, for simply sitting at His feet and listening to Him. 'Martha, Martha, you are careful and troubled about many things, but one thing is needful: and Mary has chosen that good part, which shall not be taken away from her.' The metaphorical food that Mary receives is more lasting than the food that Martha is busy preparing.

We can take from the Gospels, therefore, the message that we shouldn't be fussy about food. When challenged about eating with unwashed hands, after all, Jesus responds in Luke 11, 'give alms of what you have, and behold all things are clean to you.' What you do for others is more important than what you eat, or the appearance of cleanliness. According to Mark (chapter 7), Jesus goes on to clarify that 'there is nothing from outside a man, that entering into him can defile him: but the things which come out of him, these are they that defile the man.' The Jewish leaders who had criticised Him and His disciples were worked up about rules regarding washing and eating, to appear outwardly clean and righteous, but in God's eyes it's what's inside that counts: whether we have love in our hearts, or not.

So can we take from this that anything goes regarding food and drink? That seems to have been the traditional Christian response. Whilst Jews do not eat pork, Christians except in times of fasting traditionally have done so. Muslims do not drink alcohol; for Christians there has seldom been any such prohibition – far from it. This all relates to the Christian idea that faith is not fundamentally about religion: that love is more important than fixed rules of 'should' and 'should not'.

However, this is not necessarily what Jesus meant. One of His main themes in His teaching is that the Jewish people ought to obey the heart of the Law rather than the letter of the Law, as is well known. The

Law He refers to is of course the Law of Moses, given by God through Moses during the journey from the slavery of Egypt to the Promised Land of the Israelites, ancestors to His own Jewish people, as recounted in the first five books of the Old Testament (The Torah). That means that we ought to interpret the law – which contains many stipulations about animals that can and cannot be eaten, for instance – in accordance with what lies at its heart, the so-called 'Golden Rule': love God with all your heart, and love your neighbour as yourself.

Interpreting the law like this means getting our priorities straight, for example by avoiding the shameful situation of the priest in the parable of the Good Samaritan, recorded in Luke 10. This priest dare not help a stranger who is clearly in great need and in danger of death, for fear of falling foul of the law that forbade the priest from touching the blood of a human lest he become 'unclean'. Yet this does not mean abandoning the Law of Moses entirely: if the Golden Rule was good enough on its own, why would God bother with the rest? The Law of Moses was intended to show the Israelites how to love God and one another in their particular circumstances, a law intended to be obeyed by the whole populace.

Christianity constitutes in some sense the extension of the Jewish faith in God to the whole world, combined with the belief that the Jewish Messiah has come in the form of Jesus Christ. That means extending it to a variety of peoples in a variety of diverse circumstances, and requires a reinterpretation of the Jewish religion (rules and rituals) to meet these different circumstances. That's what Jesus was referring to when He talked about the need to put 'new wine into new bottles' – new religion is needed for a new faith. It doesn't mean no rules at all; it means that we all need to be diligent in setting our own smaller rules and boundaries in the ways we live our lives that enable us to keep the Golden Rule in our own particular circumstances.

What, then, of the rules about food and drink? The early Apostles came to the conclusion, when it became clear that Christianity was to be a faith of non-Jews as well as Jewish Christians, that non-Jewish converts should not be made to keep the Law of Moses, but must merely 'abstain from the pollutions of idols, and from things strangled, and from blood,' as recounted in Acts 15. Thus, their interpretation was that the Gentiles (those not of Jewish descent, which would include nearly all Christians nowadays) should follow the examples and teaching of Jesus, in accordance with the Golden Rule, and that these four parts of the law were of such importance that they should obey them too.

All of these rules are about food – not eating food that has been offered in sacrifice to idols, not eating animals that have been strangled to death, and not eating blood. Leviticus, that ancient book of the Law, is indeed especially damning on this point: 'whatsoever person it is that eats any kind of blood, that soul shall be cut off from his people' (Leviticus 7). Hence, the Apostles surmised that some guidance was still required regarding what you eat to avoid sinfulness in the circumstances of the Gentile converts at the time. It is needful to respect each creature God has made, in whose blood is its very life, by not eating blood. The whole law, now fulfilled in Jesus, need not be placed like a yoke about the necks of all Christians to come, as it was only ever intended for the Jewish people; but the heart of the law must be kept by every Christian, and that must entail some rules.

In our own age more than ever, different people live in different circumstances, and to enforce strict rules about the dos and don'ts of food and drink would be firmly against the spirit of Christianity. However, we are all today facing an environmental crisis of unprecedented severity, and so the sorts of rules that we all ought to follow in order to be in keeping with the Golden Rule must take this into account. In Jesus' time, the main moral questions relating to food were about how much thought we gave to the selfish pursuit of our own sustenance, and what different sorts of foods signified – 'clean' and 'unclean' animals that could and could not be eaten for instance. Such rules still apply in our culture today, as there are some animals that people eat and some which it is not considered acceptable to eat.

Yet on top of this, food has come to involve much broader moral questions today regarding the welfare of other animals and other people affected by its production in an industrialised age. Such questions must, then, be addressed alongside the others if our consumption of food is to be moral and acceptable to God.

In an age of mass-production, where foods are transported sometimes thousands of miles, farmed by labourers living in a land that the consumers of the food will never see, the everyday choices that we make about food and drink can have far-reaching consequences of which we may not be immediately aware. Originally a localised way of life through which human populations were able to feed themselves, farming has become a money-making global industry in which most of the work is either outsourced to the poor living abroad, or carried out by vast machines used by a minority in relatively wealthy parts of the world. A typical European country might have nowadays just five per cent of people employed in farming, where many countries in Africa have eighty per cent of the adult population working the land. These are often smallholder farmers or labourers carrying out the menial manual work of agriculture. Much of what is eaten by wealthier nations – especially luxury items that cannot be grown in temperate climates for much of the year – ultimately depends upon this impoverished workforce.

    One of the easiest ways that individual Christians and churches can make good choices acceptable to God regarding food, then, is to only use luxury ingredients imported from impoverished parts of the world if they are from ethically assured sources. Tea, coffee, sugar, chocolate and bananas are key examples. None of these is essential to life, and all of them are used in vast quantities by the wealthy of the world but are grown primarily by the poor. A Christian who cares for God's children must strive to ensure that they do not enjoy luxuries produced at the expense of others' suffering. A simple, effective choice is therefore to buy

Fairtrade accredited supplies of these ingredients, which means that producers are treated with dignity, paid a fair price and live and work in safe and relatively pleasant conditions. Without this accreditation, the labourers producing what we consume could quite possibly be living in squalor, working in drudgery, treated little better than slaves by big businesses exploiting cheap labour.

As Christians, we have a duty, therefore, to make the simple sacrifice of seeking out and potentially paying more for Fairtrade produce, and if it is not available making the sacrifice to forgo luxury ingredients altogether. If the whole Church throughout the world did this, there would be great incentive for Fairtrade to expand to increasing numbers of farms and labourers, improving conditions for the poorest everywhere.

Then, there is the question of what we eat. Originally, 'meat' was a general term for 'food', but has come to mean in common parlance the flesh of animals. That is not the meaning that the translators of the King James Version of the Bible had in mind with the phraseology 'life is more than meat'. The only 'meat' in the modern sense that Jesus and His followers appear to eat in the Gospels is in fact fish, which, as is obvious from the Gospel accounts, was a staple food at the time. Catching fish was used as a metaphor for inviting people into the faith when Simon and Andrew were called by Jesus as described in Mark 1:17, 'come ye after me, and I will make you to become fishers of men.' Given that Christians are commanded to love each other – including those converts we have 'caught' – the metaphor is only effective if the fisherman has respect for his fish. If he ruthlessly exploits the fish, with an industrial trawler for example, the metaphor of fishing for people becomes abhorrent.

Therefore, Jesus' attitude toward fish – creatures made by God after all – must have been at least a thankful one, even if it was necessary to kill and eat some of the fish in order to survive. Jesus used fish to sustain crowds of followers when He fed miraculously thousands of people – an event captured in all four Gospels, and sometimes recorded as having happened twice – as well as that other staple of the time, bread. Jesus also ate fish Himself after the Resurrection, according to Luke 24:42, thus proving that He was risen as a body with bodily needs; and He fed His disciples fish according to John 21 after helping them to catch so many that their nets nearly broke.

It is clear, then, that there is no universal rule against eating fish for Christians. Yet nor is it necessarily right and just, or expedient to do so. Jesus lived in a time when the human population was much smaller, the number of fish caught was much smaller, and fish populations around the world would have been more or less healthy. The devastation wrought by modern industrialised fishing techniques had not yet destroyed or endangered marine ecosystems; fish was largely local (unless salted for transport inland) and sustainable. How different is the situation today. There is little reverence, respect or thankfulness evidenced by the trawler ships that stalk our oceans, gobbling up fish in their millions for human consumption and carelessly killing other marine animals in their huge nets. Fishing has become a profit-hungry industry greedily exploiting our planet.

Some fishing can be done sustainably, but at a time when global demand is higher than can be supplied by sustainable means – and rising – it cannot be good stewardship of the Earth for us to be part of the demand. According to the Global Education Project, the fraction of wild fish stocks within biologically sustainable levels dropped from 90 per cent to 67 per cent between 1974 and 2015, and global demand is rising faster than population growth.

Nor is farmed fish the answer: here, fish are trapped unnaturally in an artificial environment, fed with food that is seldom sustainable (often other fish) and produce copious quantities of pollution. The fish are susceptible to all sorts of diseases that free-swimming fish would not be. This fish farming is not a loving, Christian way to treat other animals, and is a far cry from the small-scale fishing of Jesus' day. Unless we live in a coastal community dependent upon small-scale sustainable fishing, like Jesus did, eating fish – free or farmed – is therefore not at the current time a Christian thing to do. In other words, if He lived in our own age, Christ would not likely have been buying fish from the supermarket. It is a healthy, nutritious food, in moderate quantities. But it must be given up if we care about the health of Earth's oceans.

Interestingly, it was not fish that Jesus used to represent His body at the Last Supper. Nor was it any other kind of flesh such as that of a lamb, which would have been the obvious option if he was following the example of the Jewish Passover meal. It was bread, plain and simple bread – the true staple food for so much of the world for so long. We pray 'give us this day our daily bread' in the Lord's Prayer, in part evoking the desire for Christ's body to sustain us spiritually just as bread sustains us physically. Jesus has replaced the old Jewish rituals of animal sacrifice with one of bread – a plant-based sacrifice if you will. His body is slain so that no other blood need be shed – the eating of bread to remember Him is sufficient.

Indeed, there is no reference in any of the Gospels to Christ or any of His disciples eating any animal flesh at all, aside from fish. Jesus' abolition of animal sacrifice can be seen as an abolition of eating animal flesh entirely, again except fish. There is no longer any need to slay the best of the flocks in sacrifice to God, to atone for eating the rest of the flocks – His creatures – ourselves, which is part of what the animal sacrifice rituals were about. Certainly, Christ makes the shedding of animal blood unnecessary, even if it does not become unlawful: there is no law for Christians except the law of love, which we must show to all fellow creatures if we are to be stewards of the Earth. And we know that eating the flesh of animals not only entails taking those animals' lives unnecessarily, but also has today profound consequences for the health of our planet and its inhabitants.

It is estimated that around one third of global greenhouse gas emissions come from agriculture, and the vast majority of those emissions come from animal agriculture. Because eating animal flesh is so much less efficient as a source of calories than eating plant matter directly, huge amounts of land must be set aside to graze animals that could otherwise be restored to nature or used to grow crops. This drives deforestation, especially in the Amazon region where it is cattle ranches that are responsible for much of the forest clearance. Cows, sheep and other ruminants themselves produce methane, a very potent greenhouse gas. Although methane is short-lived in the atmosphere, as is often pointed out, it is less often noted that it is naturally converted into carbon dioxide, which is certainly not short-lived. Even if some meat production can be done sustainably – a certain amount of grass-fed beef in the UK, for instance – again the earth's capacity to produce animals for human consumption sustainably is limited, and any contribution we make to the global demand for animal flesh therefore contributes to the problem. From an environmental perspective, it is therefore our duty as stewards of creation to refrain wherever possible from eating meat, or at least to eat it only on rare occasions, as was usually the case for most people for thousands of years before the twentieth century explosion in meat consumption. Were that explosion to be repeated across the world, and 8 billion people began to eat meat on the scale of modern-day westerners, it would be impossible to prevent catastrophic climate change and ecosystem destruction.

    Whatever one's stance on this issue, it is indubitable that eating animal flesh has severe environmental and ethical implications, with more moral cost per kilogram than any other foods. It is perfectly possible to live healthily and happily without ever eating animal flesh of any kind, and to get protein instead from plant-based sources such as soya, or a moderate amount of sustainably, locally and ethically produced eggs and dairy produce. If Christians are serious about our vocation to steward the planet, to feed the hungry and to share Earth's resources fairly, then, we must be careful to avoid eating animal flesh wherever possible. This is the single biggest thing we can do as individuals to make a difference for good to the health of our environment and other people.

3

The Body is More than Raiment

> Consider the lilies how they grow: they toil not, they spin not, and yet I say unto you, that Solomon in all his glory was not arrayed as one of these. (Luke 12:27)

With these words Jesus continues the parable we saw begun in the last chapter. Flowers, He reminds us, are very short-lived – and yet so beautiful that no human art can match them.

This remains the case today, when our innate yearning for the beauty of nature cannot be satisfied by any projected image created by mankind, nor by the ugly metropolises we construct around ourselves. And if those fleeting wonders of nature we admire can be created so beautifully by God, will He not be able to clothe us with beauty also? God makes the flowers of the Earth beautiful through no effort on their part, and Jesus' point is that, since God loves us so much, He will surely put even more effort into making us look beautiful – with no work required on our part either. Indeed, the flowers soon fade away and are destroyed; their beauty is but a memory. If Christ promises to the faithful everlasting life, how much more worthwhile is God's work to clothe us in finery?

Now, it is quite evident that not all human beings look beautiful in their own eyes, or even in the eyes of other humans. There is seldom an eye more judgemental of one's appearance than one's own. For as long as we can remember, humans have tried to make ourselves look more beautiful with the aid of fine clothing, makeup and even physical interventions. Beauty is, though, a subjective quality, and what is beautiful to one person may not be so to another, or could change over time. There was a time when ladies having extremely small feet was considered beautiful by the elites in China, and painful was the effort to try to enforce this 'beauty' upon young girls. There was a time when the whitest skin was considered 'beautiful' in European culture, and poisonous powders were applied to the skin to whiten it with deleterious results. More recently, tanned skin was more in vogue, and countless cases of skin cancer have resulted from efforts to procure this effect through tanning salons or prolonged bathing under a hot Sun.

We are all well aware of the harmful and sometimes even fatal effect that media images of supposedly 'beautiful' people can have, especially on teenagers and young adults who feel that they do not conform to the modern-day conception of 'beauty' and its reliance upon being thin and perfectly formed. Whole industries have developed in the modern world that draw profit from exploiting a desire to look more handsome – ranging from cosmetic surgery to tooth-whitening toothpaste. All of them reinforce and rely upon the sentiment, encouraged by social media, that 'I am ugly – make me beautiful!'

Jesus' words, then, stand in stark contrast to the modern conception of beauty. Jesus was speaking to people who could not afford makeup and for whom perfume was a precious commodity – hence the furore amongst His disciples when Mary 'wasted' a whole pound of ointment in anointing Jesus' feet (John 12:3). They would seldom have obtained new clothes, and the ones they had would likely be rough and plain. Those who wore soft garments, Jesus Himself pointed out, dwelt in 'king's houses' (Matthew 11:8). Without modern dental care, albeit also without modern-day access to sugary foods, their teeth would hardly have been pristine, and rough work in the harsh conditions of summer and winter may well have aged their skin. Yet for all this, Jesus told them, they were each one made more beautiful than the lilies, which were themselves more beautiful than the famously wealthy king Solomon's clothing.

How could this be? Jesus' conception of beauty was clearly less fickle than that of most people, then or now. He wouldn't have had to tell the parable at all if his audience weren't concerned with outward appearance and didn't desire, if they could, to wear the beautiful clothing of the rich. Jesus knew that such clothing would not last; its beauty was ephemeral, as is the beauty bought through expensive makeup or cosmetic surgery – which can leave people looking rather different to what they intended anyway, when the rest of their body ages around the facelift or Botox. It may be a cliché, but for

The Body is More than Raiment

Jesus we are each beautiful just the way God made us – that is to say, just the way we truly are. It doesn't matter whether we have wrinkly skin, missing teeth, pimples, deformities, even missing limbs. Jesus looks at us through the eyes of love, like a parent who looks upon a beloved child and thinks it to be the most beautiful creature in the world.

Jesus sees into our hearts, and there He sees beauty; He looks into our bodies, and there He sees beauty, for we are each of us unique and precious creations of God. It is only our sin, our selfishness, our turning away from God – and, yes, our labelling of ourselves and others unfairly – that makes us ugly. Turn to God, enter His kingdom, and we each become all beauty not by changing who we are or how we look but by embracing fully our true selves, and all we were always meant to be.

If the Christian realises this – truly realises this – then he or she is set free from the desire to obtain superficial beauty in the eyes of the world, or to fuss about new clothes or cosmetics. It isn't that we don't need clothing that is clean and warm – or cool, as the case may be – and Jesus Himself reassures us that 'your Father knoweth that ye have need of these things' (Luke 12:30). The key point is that we should not worry, expending thought and effort needlessly, about outward appearance. Instead, we should seek 'first the kingdom of God… and all these things shall be added unto you' (Matthew 6:33). In other words, we are not to follow the latest fashions, or fret about supposed physical 'ugliness'; we are not to worry about the clothes we are to wear when we give our lives to God and set out where He sends us. For, as with food, God will provide us with what we need when it comes to clothing.

As is the case with food, though, this does not mean that Christians should take an 'anything goes' attitude towards clothing – at least, not in the context of our modern world, in which the decisions we make can have far-reaching consequences. We might have been able to take such an attitude in centuries past, when items of clothing were valued more highly, came from more sustainable sources and lasted longer than they do in our present society of fast, cheap fashion. However, nowadays, the procurement of clothing has profound ethical implications which must be taken into account if we are to live by the commandment to love our neighbours as ourselves. The 'fast fashion' of recent decades, whereby consumers are encouraged to replace perfectly good garments after using them once or perhaps even not at all in order to keep up with what is 'fashionable' – what is supposed to look 'beautiful' – in a particular season is undermining the very survival of our own society and of other species.

It is reported that the average American in 2022 bought sixty-six items of clothing per year, and threw them away at roughly the same rate – one every five days or so. Thirteen kilograms of textiles are produced globally per person per year, mostly made of cheap polyester that does not biodegrade and poses a lasting hazard to multiple life-forms, including humans, when fibres are released into the water supply from washing machines. More than ninety million tonnes of clothing are disposed of every year, some of it never worn at all but thrown away by retailers and customers because it has 'gone out of fashion'.

Fashion is a major contributor towards global greenhouse gas emissions, and polyester's main alternative – cotton – is itself very energy-hungry and water-thirsty to produce. Buying new clothes made from either material therefore contributes to a global industry that perpetuates climate change, ocean pollution, water shortages in arid cotton-growing regions and exploitative labour in sweatshops. None of this is justifiable simply to obtain additions to our wardrobes that we do not really need, just because they look nice or fit in with modern styles.

Christians, then, who care about the planet and the living conditions of other people, must be careful when it comes to buying clothing – whether personal or liturgical wear. The first and most important thing for us to do is to avoid buying new clothes at all wherever possible. Whatever the material of our existing outfits, to use them repeatedly and indeed repair them if they tear is certainly the least harmful option. The only exception to this is worn-out polyester-based items which have a particular tendency to shed fibres when washed; for this subset of clothing it might be better to get rid of it rather than try to keep wearing and repairing it.

Importantly, it should not matter to us whether our clothing is out-dated, or whether we end up wearing the same things repeatedly – because our beauty is in our faith, not in our clothing. If we must buy clothing – which, after all, does not last for ever – it is of course best to buy it second-hand, especially if one can support a good cause whilst doing so, as is the case with charity shops. The key thing – that which will actually make a difference to the environment – is to reduce the amount of clothing coming onto the market, and thus to reduce the amount of resources required to manufacture new clothes and the quantity of pollutants produced in their production, distribution and disposal. In other words we need, as a species, to make better use of a smaller amount of clothing, rather than wastefully producing far more than we actually need. There will be times where it is necessary to buy new, but it is an act of compassion towards the world to resist the temptation to do so by default, and to minimise getting new clothes wherever possible.

When we do buy new garments, it is important to consider both the materials they are made of and the conditions in which they were made. Being part of a market for polyester, and thus helping to perpetuate its use, is not good – and it may be more ethical to spend more money on a more expensive but potentially longer-lasting natural, biodegradable material than to buy synthetic alternatives that are cheap in price but costly in impact. Cotton, with its very intensely industrialised production methods, is hardly any better when it comes to carbon emissions – though at least it does biodegrade and is not such a danger to other species or our own health (the health effects of ingesting tiny particles of polyester shed from clothes are not yet clear). There is such a thing as sustainably-sourced cotton, though it is unlikely that the whole world's clothing needs could be made from cotton sustainably, given that the cotton plant only grows well in certain places and potentially competes with food crops. Hence, cotton is better, but not ideal.

Better than both is sustainably-sourced wool, which can be harvested without harming the animal that grows it: indeed, sheep need to be shorn in the summer months for their own welfare. To waste such a natural, versatile, biodegradable material would surely be a travesty. At the same time, ruminant animals such as sheep must be limited in number because they produce copious emissions of methane, a potent greenhouse gas. Using the wool from existing flocks of sheep hence makes sense, but bringing more sheep into the world simply to harvest their fleeces does not. Again, the quantity of truly sustainable wool is limited in the long-term, though in today's circumstances – there are already millions of sheep in the UK, needing to be shorn – it is a good option to choose.

Perhaps the most sustainable material for clothing is hemp, which grows easily in temperate regions such as Britain and which was once used much more widely than it is now to produce linen. Growing a crop such as hemp draws down carbon from the atmosphere, which ends up being locked into the clothes ultimately produced from it. This means that, if managed properly and used to feed local need, the production of hemp clothing can be carbon neutral. If overall meat consumption is reduced, freeing up farmland to grow hemp without impacting the availability of food crops, hemp could be a viable solution to the clothing needs of the future.

God will, after all, provide clothing for everyone without harming anyone in the process – if only we have the grace to accept what He gives us and distribute our resources fairly. By choosing more sustainable options for clothing, and refusing to follow the fast fashion of a fickle throw-away culture, Christians can begin to make a difference for the good of our neighbours in space and time. If we are content with what we have, and set our hearts to seek the Kingdom of God, God will give us what we need. Flashy designs and varied colours, though espoused by the modern consumer age, are not necessary to our mission as Christ's followers. They often require materials and dyes that cause harm. These unnecessary luxuries must not be allowed to become the cause of our sin or barriers to our doing good in the world. Nor, for that matter, should needless cosmetics.

A 'cosmetic' can be defined as a substance applied to the skin solely to improve its appearance. By 'cosmetic' here we do not, therefore, refer to any product that is necessary to health – moisturising creams might, for example, be necessary to avoid dry or itchy skin and would not be included in our definition, although ethical considerations should still be made when using such products. Cosmetics have the sole function of making us look other than we actually are, and in light of Christ's conception of beauty they are hence wholly unnecessary to the Christian. This does not mean that cosmetics should never be used as an absolute rule, but rather that they should not be used at the expense of the wellbeing

The Body is More than Raiment

of others. Cosmetics made from sustainable resources tested only on willing participants and manufactured in a way that provides a good living for people are probably not a bad thing, so long as their use does not lead to vanity or a false emphasis on the importance of outward 'beauty'.

Unfortunately, however, few cosmetics fall under these criteria. Many are made using oil, are tested on unwitting animals alongside other potentially more harmful alternatives that could produce horrendous pain, and are manufactured in factories in parts of the world notorious for poor working conditions. If such products only provide superficial benefits, for all this harm, then to use them cannot be the loving thing to do.

Jesus tells another parable about the sorts of clothes that He wants us to put on. In Matthew 22, He speaks of a king holding a banquet to which, when the initial guest-list refuse to come, all and sundry are apparently invited. It is clear from the context that this banquet represents God's Kingdom, into which now all people – not only Jews but also Gentiles – are invited. The twist in the tale comes when the king notices 'a man which had not on a wedding garment' (Matthew 22:11), a person who is not, in other words, properly dressed for the Kingdom of God. This man is thrown out, 'into outer darkness'. Now, the implication of this is surely not that people who dress wrongly at wedding banquets get thrown out of the party; the problem with the man in the story was not his literal clothing. Jesus teaches us that we are to clothe ourselves beautifully not with fabric but with righteousness, not with cosmetics that cover up our physical defects but with a love that cleanses us of our spiritual ugliness.

We must, therefore, as Christians refuse to waste our time here in Earth worrying about our physical appearance, or accumulating clothes that we do not use simply to store them in a wardrobe at great cost to the environment. As Jesus Himself points out in Matthew 6:19, they will only get eaten up by moths. What benefit is this to anybody? We must refuse to comply with a dangerous cultural shift towards the over-use of cosmetics and needless plastic surgery. Any beauty that we can achieve through these works of man is as transitory as a dandelion or a daisy, a flash of colour that soon blows away in the wind (see Psalm 103).

Instead, we can trust God to create all such aesthetic beauty, delighting in each creature He has made just as we are – short, tall, fat, thin, and regardless of any disability. Wear clothes that do the job of keeping us warm and decent and which are suited to the occasion in hand, and be satisfied. We should spend our time cultivating the spiritual beauty through which we can truly shine – the smiles on our faces, the joy that pours forth from our lips, the love that works through our limbs, and the faith that guides our feet. Then, we shall be well-dressed for the banquet of Heaven, and we shall lay up treasures of great beauty in Heaven, because our lives will look just as God intended them to.

4

The House on the Rock

> Whosoever cometh to me, and heareth my sayings, and doeth them, I will shew you to whom he is like. He is like a man which built an house, and digged deep, and laid the foundation on a rock: and when the flood arose, the stream beat vehemently upon that house, and could not shake it: for it was founded upon a rock. But he that heareth, and doeth not, is like a man that without a foundation built an house upon the earth; against which the stream did beat vehemently, and immediately it fell; and the ruin of that house was great. (Luke 6:47-49)

Everyone knows that a poorly-built building is an accident waiting to happen. Put up a house with flimsy walls and no foundations, and it is likely to collapse, get blown over in a gale or be washed away in a flood. Even a tent needs ropes and pegs to keep it dependently upright; if you don't bother using them, you might get away with it for a few hours in calm, fine conditions but you won't fare well in a storm. You will have built no lasting settlement.

When Jesus uses the metaphor of the house built on the sand and the house built on the rock, recorded in

Luke 6, He is of course referring not to physical foundations but to His listeners' spiritual foundations. If you have a fickle faith – built on sand – it might hold up for a while, when things are going well, but it's really only talk without any substance. For faith to survive and to support you, holding you upright when things get tough, it needs to be built upon a rock – firm foundations that won't simply totter. Jesus is the rock on which true faith is built, the 'stone that the builders rejected' that becomes the 'chief cornerstone' as He described Himself according to Luke 20:17, quoting Psalm 118. Likewise, His close disciple Peter (a name that literally means 'stone') is the 'rock' upon whom the whole Church will be built according to Matthew 16:18. The parable, then, is about faith – a spiritual House, not a physical building.

Yet Jesus was able to utilise this metaphor precisely because the importance of building a physical house properly was well-known. In a region not immune to earthquakes, it would be obvious that failing to fix firm foundations could be fatal. Buildings have to be planned and carefully made, a truth undoubtedly of no less importance in our own day than it was in His. As the population increases and the demand for consumer goods and home comforts rises globally, it is vital that new buildings are carefully constructed, and that old ones are safely and efficiently utilised. If we love our neighbours, we should want them to live in safe and pleasant homes. If we care about the stewardship of creation, we should be concerned that homes for humans and all our other buildings do not erode the habitats of species that live alongside us any further than is already the case in our hugely built-upon world, let alone render the Earth uninhabitable to humans and others by driving climate change.

Whenever a building is erected where one wasn't there before, a piece of land is taken for our own, human use. There is not necessarily anything wrong with this, so long as we recognise that this land is not truly our own: in fact, it belongs to God, as does the whole Earth, and we as wayfarers have taken use of it only for a time. Several moral obligations, for Christians, spring from this – in light of our belief that God loves His creation and that we are merely its stewards, not its masters.

The first and most obvious is that because our building takes away land that would otherwise have been, or had the potential to be, other species' habitat, we should not erect buildings or concrete-over areas of land unnecessarily. God provides for our need, and wants us to share in such a way as to meet one another's needs, but He does not provide for our greed, which by its very nature deprives others needlessly of life. Therefore, it is important to encourage the use of existing buildings before constructing new ones, unless the older ones are unusable. Churches and individual Christians should consider this, as well as wider society: if we are to be stewards of creation, we must protect other creatures' homes from being destroyed merely on the basis of whim or greed. Those new buildings that are constructed should be placed where they will do the least damage to nature or to other people – preferably on 'brownfield' sites that have already been built on before.

Clearing a 'slum' of thousands of people to make way for a posh apartment block that none of these people can afford to, or would want to, live in is clearly unjust, as is chopping down a wood to build a shopping centre. Yet these sorts of things were done in the name of 'progress' not many years ago. Christians must oppose such developments.

A second imperative is to build or repair using the most sustainable materials and methods possible, which do not do disproportionate harm to other people in their procurement or come from delicate ecosystems such as rainforests or non-renewable resources that will run out in the near future. Most Christians are not architects or property developers or officials with the power to impose regulations on builders, of course. But we may be in a position, on the church council or in our own home, that requires us to engage with such issues. Using sustainable materials – such as responsibly-sourced wood, which stores carbon rather than releasing it – and avoiding concrete, the use of which is the cause of a sizeable proportion of global greenhouse gas emissions, may be a more expensive option. Yet if the true costs of using oil-based materials, concrete and metal is taken into account, it becomes obvious that sustainable materials are much more ethical choices and, in the long-term, are much cheaper.

How can we, as a Church, literally build our house using iron ore that has been dug from a voluminous pit somewhere in China by workers whose very lives are endangered daily by their work? Or concrete and steel, when producing them involves pouring out such pollution as to endanger the lives of millions? Such a moral imperative did not exist in Jesus' day, when there was little option other than to use local, sustainable materials to build most dwellings – unless you were a king, pharaoh or emperor who could command an army of slaves to haul in goods from far away. For us today, the impacts of the building materials we choose have the potential to be much greater, and the issue should be much more at the forefront of our minds. Buildings tend to be long-lasting and so, often, is their effect on the wider environment. We should always be looking to the long-term and asking, what effect will this building have on the world of the future, in decades to come?

Too many people have failed to ask themselves this question, leading to thousands of now-hideous concrete monstrosities from the 1960s and 70s that nobody should have to live in; to dangerous buildings like the Grenfell Tower that burnt down in 2017; and to ugly industrial and residential estates that scar God's beautiful creation. In some places, these continue to be flung up, using cheap materials that have a profound environmental impact.

We should, then, build less, and choose carefully what materials we build with, both as a society and as individuals. But another moral calling for the Christian is to ensure that the buildings that we already have and any that we build in the future are managed in such a way as to benefit and not degrade the local and global environment. There is much to be said for the 'Eco Church' movement, intended to encourage churches to strive to be more sustainable by cutting energy use and making churchyards more hospitable for nature, for example – and also, importantly, by preaching the message of sustainable living. Christianity runs through our entire lives, as Christians, not just our time in church. It is important for us to manage our own homes, as well as our churches, in a way that allows other beings to flourish. We can do this in big ways and small.

A small thing like switching off electrical devices when they're not in use to save energy probably doesn't make much difference on its own. Yet it is a prayer to God – a small sacrifice even – which when magnified across many millions of people would make a very big difference indeed. Additionally, many people cannot afford to be wasteful of energy anyway, and if we are not amongst them, being careful with what energy we use is a voluntary poverty that puts us in solidarity with the poor even if it is of little direct help.

The big issue regarding energy and buildings at present is that of how to heat them, given that the gas and oil so widely used for this purpose are finite, increasingly expensive and powerful contributors to climate change. How much we can do individually to swap these fossil fuels for more sustainable alternatives such as heat pumps depends on our financial situations, at least in the present political circumstances. Certainly, moving away from fossil fuels should be done wherever possible, and it is important that new gas and oil boilers are discouraged even if they are cheaper than greener options. The easiest and most efficient way to reduce emissions, though, is to prayerfully make the sacrifice of slightly cooler living conditions, opting for the jumper over the radiator – within reason! This is not a call to opt for unhealthily and unpleasantly cold living conditions, nor is it an excuse for involuntarily cold houses caused by fuel poverty, which remains a serious issue even in our 'advanced' civilisation. Rather, it is a call for those who can afford to heat their buildings not to do so to unnecessary levels.

To ensure that we do not waste what we use, but use it for the genuine good, is the important principle here. Similarly, it may be both expensive and a waste of resources to replace old single-glaze glass with double-glazing, especially where windows are not especially large or there is historic architecture to consider. Simply turning down the thermostat to 17°C – a very liveable temperature – saves a lot of energy compared to 20°C without all the emissions associated with ripping out and replacing windows. In churches, obviously the latter option is seldom a possibility anyway, and if the building is only to be used for a few hours per week it makes financial and environmental sense to only heat it to a moderate temperature in cold weather, even if that means coats staying on.

Perhaps more important still than our small contribution to the global fight against climate change is the difference that Christians and churches can make to our own local environment. Cutting greenhouse gas emissions and using sustainable resources is a prayer, and a drop in the ocean that undoubtedly we must contribute if we are to help turn the tide on climate change. But to look after the environment on our own doorstep – and, indeed, on our own buildings themselves – is an act of love and compassion towards other individuals with whom we share our living space, both human and non-human. To fulfil our calling to be good stewards, we must allow and enable all life to thrive insofar as we possibly can.

Gardens, therefore, should not be carefully manicured and tightly controlled – or, still worse, replaced by concrete or artificial grass. These give rise to dead spaces, where very little can live. Nor should we be using herbicides and pesticides to kill plants and animals that might otherwise thrive. Yes, planting ornamental flowers is often a good thing if they are sourced sustainably, especially if they are beloved of insects which we need for pollination as well as for their own sakes as part of the wonder of God's creation. Yes, we must weed, we must dig, we must cut and trim and prune to keep a garden healthy and well-balanced and to prevent one or other plant from taking over (thistles and brambles for instance) to the detriment of everything else. Especially in graveyards, it is important that things do not become overgrown or inaccessible. Yet at the same time, allowing nature the space to grow and to thrive is one of the best things we can do to improve the quality of life on our planet.

Let the grass grow long, with paths running through for access, and cut it down only twice a year – preferably with a scythe to prevent harm to any animals that may be hiding therein. Then, wild flowers have the chance to grow up, butterflies, dragonflies and other insects have somewhere to live and multiply, and the carbon emissions and dreadful noise pollution of the lawnmower and strimmer are replaced by the carbon-absorbing capacity of a rich ecosystem. We can use our own gardens and churchyards to help reverse a decades-long decline in wildflower meadows and inspect populations. Furthermore, in those places that we do cut short (and it is natural and good to have variety in our gardens) we can provide havens for birds – bird baths, feeders and nest boxes – which are sure to win the favour of avian visitors wherever we are situated.

Both noise and light pollution are unfortunately too often ignored and left unchecked in our towns – and increasingly our countryside too. Day by day, the peace of the world is broken by the noise of destruction, as loud petrol-powered implements rip up grasses, 'weeds' and hedges. Rather than bringing in all this polluting modern machinery, it is more in keeping with care for God's creation – and for one's neighbours – to use a scythe or a pair of sheers, or even to opt for electric cutting equipment – all can do the job just as well without the smoke and the noise. Leaf-blowers are a particularly unnecessary menace, doing a job that a good broom or a rake could accomplish in the same amount of time without making such a din. It is incumbent upon us all too choose such gentler, kinder methods of working with nature, rather than attacking it full-on. Meanwhile, security lights on houses and churches, though perhaps useful for dark winter evenings when people will be attending church, can be very harmful to wildlife when left active all the time. Bright lights suddenly coming on at night can confuse insects, and effectively destroy bats' habitat by making it impossible for them to fly and hunt by night. Switching to LEDs makes the situation even worse, as these more closely mimic daylight than conventional sodium lamps. External lights of any kind also add to the light pollution that prevents us all from enjoying the wonder of the night sky, and should be avoided wherever possible.

None of this is expensive or difficult – helping insects and birds to thrive is as easy as it is rewarding. In large part it involves just letting things be rather than always trying to 'tidy up' and interfere with our outdoor spaces. If the funds and the space are available, a step further is to plant more trees – in appropriate places, of course. Trees are wonderful beings, sucking in copious carbon dioxide, providing a home for insects and birds and in many cases providing fruit that serves as food either for us or for them. The more native trees we all plant, the more emissions are 'offset' and the greener our country becomes. Once, Britain was covered with forest; now only about one eighth of our land is forested. Whatever we as Christians can do to restore trees and avoid cutting existing ones down is a step towards a better prospect for our local ecosystems.

Nor need support for nature stop in the soil that surrounds our buildings. Instead of seeing buildings as private homes for mankind, where nature is excluded, there would be great benefit in seeing these, too, as part of the landscape entrusted to us by God. Just because we live inside buildings, that doesn't mean that nature must be excluded from the outside. Indeed, buildings so often get in the way of animals needing to move across what was once their habitat; making these buildings nature-friendly can re-open those routes and restore the habitability of the towns, cities and villages humans have built.

Some years ago now, there was a lot of hype about 'green walls' that could support a variety of plants. Many of these did not last very well, and they can be cumbersome to construct, let alone to keep watered. But the principle of allowing plants to colonise and surround our buildings is a sound one, allowing insects and other, smaller animals to live in close proximity to us. Obviously, structural reasons dictate that large plants such as trees should not be placed very close to buildings, but planting something such as a shallow-rooted bush or a climbing plant next to walls transforms them from dead places to living ones, with very little expertise required. This may not be something for older, listed buildings but more modern churches, church halls and houses could quickly and easily benefit from such planting.

Similarly, whilst 'green walls' may not be especially effective, so-called 'green roofs' can be very beneficial. Wherever buildings have flat roofs, this technique involves simply planting them up with relatively lightweight greenery, which provides splashes of colour in an otherwise drab environment and another stepping-stone habitat for species to cross our cities and towns. Placing plants in containers is an easy way to achieve this, turning buildings into living landscapes and, potentially, carbon sinks rather than carbon sources.

The important point to take from all this is that the Earth is our living home, to be shared with many other living creatures. We should treat no part of it as worthy of being dead and lifeless – whether bare concrete or plastic grass or drab, grey streets. If we let climbing plants cover that concrete, replace that plastic grass with real grass or moss and let it grow and fill with flowers, and plant trees along that street, we are no longer stealing land from other species and making it our own, sole, diminished abode. Instead, we are living alongside and amongst the other species God has made and loves, and we live in a beautiful paradise of life rather than an ugly cityscape of death.

So, the rule is, plant – and allow to grow. We may not as individual Christians have much say in how a whole town or city or country looks and feels, lives and breathes. But we can allow our little portions – our homes, our halls, our churchyards – to brim with life, and undo some of the encroachment of cold concrete that recent decades have seen. This is living out powerfully our Christian calling to steward the Earth; this is putting into practice our Christian love for God and His whole, wonderful creation. It is also a means to fight climate change, provide habitat and make the places we live in beautiful and full of life. It is about sustainability for the future, making a world that future generations will enjoy living in, not a concrete metropolis that repulses us with its crumbling, rotting, artificial edifices. That is what is means to build our houses not on the sand, but on the rock.

5

Lambs among Wolves

> Go your ways: behold I send you forth as lambs among wolves. Carry neither purse, not script, nor shoes: and salute no man by the way. And into whatsoever house ye enter, first say, 'Peace be to this house.'
> (Luke 10:3-5)

These, according to Luke, are the words with which Jesus sent out seventy of His followers in pairs to carry out His work of healing and proclaiming the Good News that God's Kingdom has arrived.

These disciples were on a special mission, not to be distracted from their purpose – and one that was limited in duration. It does not seem likely that Jesus is asking all His followers throughout all time to act in exactly the same way whenever we go on journeys. Yet He is, clearly, setting an example here, one which we all might do well to bear in mind when we travel. Not least, we should ask ourselves what are we travelling for, what do we need to bring, and what will be the effect of our journey on those whom we meet on the way or at our destination? Will we, in our words, in the way we act and in our very presence perhaps, proclaim the Word of God and our joy to be part of God's Kingdom? Will we bring healing through our presence? Or might we bring hurt?

As Christians, we need to be aware that every journey we make is meaningful – whether we travel as pilgrims to far-flung lands, go on holiday, or simply set off down the street on our way to work. We have been entrusted with a precious gift – the Word of God, the truth that Christ Himself testified to us – and it is in going out into the world, in whatever capacity, that we have the opportunity to live out this Word and share it with others, if we choose to do so.

Travel in our own time is very different to what Jesus' followers would have experienced. In fact, it is difficult to think of an aspect of our lives that has changed more radically since that time. What a picture of simplicity it seems, to read Jesus' instructions to the seventy: going out on foot in their pairs, barefooted or in sandals, no bag or money to weigh them down or worry their hearts. It would certainly be difficult to go on a long journey like this today, and clearly the climate of first-century Judea is not enjoyed by all parts of the world: we are not intended to make such a trek, or to try and apply the disciples' example literally in the midst of a British winter. Yet there is something to be said for the simplicity of walking, and something to be said for not going alone and not being encumbered by too much baggage.

There are many reasons why we travel today, just as there were in Jesus' time. Jesus Himself spent much of His ministry moving from place to place, bringing healing to those whom He met: and not only in

Judea, His people's homeland, or in Galilee where He was brought up. Jesus also travelled to Samaria, the descendent of the old Kingdom of Israel after it split from Judea, a place that was looked down upon by Judeans. Visits to Tyre and Sidon would have taken Him outside Jewish territory altogether into the lands of the Gentiles. One estimate puts the distance Jesus travelled in His lifetime at over twenty thousand miles, including more than three thousand during His ministry. His life began with travel, as His parents journeyed to Bethlehem for His birth before feeling to Egypt for safety, and the Magi travelled many miles to visit Him. His mission reached its climax with His travel towards Jerusalem, where His life was to come to an end.

Thus Jesus was certainly not averse to travel, and His command to His disciples at the end of Matthew's Gospel that should go and make disciples of all nations (Matthew 28:19) implies that He expected travel to be a significant part of His followers' ministry too. Nor was this unusual: although perhaps most people in those days stayed closer to home than many would today, it is clear that there were plenty of people who travelled long distances, even then. The New Testament records disciples travelling on foot from Jerusalem to Emmaus as a matter of course (Luke 24), and Paul travelling to Damascus (Acts 9), neither of which were missionary journeys. The Romans sent their legions across Europe and beyond, and the Empire would have been connected by messengers. Sailing across the Mediterranean was routine, especially in summer. Certainly, news travelled – albeit much more slowly than it might today – and goods were traded across vast distances. Ultimately, Christianity spread across the 'Old World' remarkably rapidly, aided by the trade routes and the Roman Empire.

The difference with travel today, then, is not *that* we travel or even that we travel large distances – but rather concerns the quality and quantity of the travel that we undertake. All Jesus' travels were done on foot, whether His own feet or those of a donkey. Christian missionaries would have also travelled by sailing ship – still a relatively slow method by today's standards. Of course, from the point of view of the environment, such methods would have next to no negative impact, unless perhaps the wood needed to make the ships was logged sustainably from a forest that would grow back. A lot of wood wasn't in ancient times, which is why Europe's forests were largely lost even before the medieval era, especially in Britain. But in principle, wood is a renewable and sustainable material – and indeed using it in today's context can help to lock up carbon from the atmosphere so long as trees are grown to replace those that are felled. In any case, there were no greenhouse gas emissions associated with walking or sailing, and even riding horses and donkeys hardly contributes to methane emissions as compared to keeping flocks of ruminant animals for food. The travel undertaken by the early Christians and by Christ Himself was, then, gentle on the environment – so much so that it was not an ethical question that any of them had to address.

How different things are now. Instead of occasional, purposeful journeys, most human beings today in much of the world think nothing of jumping into a car to drive a few miles – and, indeed, in some instances whole ways of life have come to depend upon it. Amenities – including churches – no longer have to be within walking distance of houses, as they would have been in the past, because of the assumption of twentieth-century planners that almost everyone would be able to drive. This same assumption has eroded local public transport links, which themselves tend to run on fossil fuels like the majority of cars. For longer journeys, it has become normal to use aeroplanes to soar across the skies at previously unimaginable speeds, travelling in hours a distance that would have taken weeks or months if it was possible at all to traverse in Jesus' time. Now, with the advent of anthropogenic climate change, and in the knowledge that these fossil fuels are finite and will be unavailable to future generations if we use them up today, the ethics of all this travel can certainly be called into question.

Even electric cars are not necessarily an answer, as they require even more resources – notably precious metals – to build than do conventional cars, requiring extensive mining that does great damage to the environment in far-flung parts of the world. Electricity also has to be produced somehow, and very few countries are anywhere near achieving one hundred per cent renewable electricity generation. Thus, our modern addiction to fast travel – to the corner shop by car or on holiday by plane – is unavoidably contributing to the vast quantities of greenhouse gasses being emitted into the atmosphere and degrading the natural world. Jesus' travel did not do this.

Yet the problem with modern travel runs much deeper than this. Over recent decades in particular, travel has come to adopt a somewhat different quality to that undertaken by Jesus. For Him, travel was all about the journey: stopping on route to spread the Good News and to heal, meeting people on the way, or going into a desert place to pray and contemplate. Yes, the ultimate destination of Jerusalem was important too, but getting there was far from the sole aim of Jesus' travels. None of this would have been possible had Jesus driven a car to Jerusalem, let alone flown in. His was a pilgrimage – as much about the journey as about the destination, which remained true for countless generations of Christian pilgrims since that time.

Today, by contrast, our lives seem to exist in order to be filled with busy-ness, and travel has therefore become too often just about getting from A to B. We want to go on holiday to southern Spain; we're not interested in spending a week travelling through France – we just want the cheapest, quickest means of getting to our destination – so we fly. We want to go to church for the 9 o' clock service; it's too far to walk in time so we drive. Too often we fail to consider the impact that these choices are making on the environment, and fail to bewail what we are losing by choosing quick, private means of transport: all the people we would otherwise meet, and all the wonders of nature we would otherwise interact with, along the way.

Lambs among Wolves

Were Jesus alive today, would He have flown in an aeroplane? Certainly not – for Jesus was poor, and the poor cannot afford plane tickets, but rather suffer the ill-effects of climate change caused by the richer inhabitants of the world. In any case, Jesus was interested in the journey, rather than the destination. Would He have driven in a car? I think seldom, if at all. There are parts of the modern world so impoverished by concrete and tarmac that no life lives there, and one might as well shoot straight along the road past such places. But in most places there are still people to meet, still miracles to behold – and, perhaps, to perform. If only we take the time to travel slowly, and interact with our surroundings.

Then we can properly engage with our planet and its people, and perceive the real needs and circumstances of those we live alongside. A digital culture has to far too great an extent closed us off from one another in the twenty-first century, and ironically the 'world wide web' has cornered us into increasingly polarised and closed-off communities of our own construction, interacting only with those who think and feel the same way as we do and vilifying everyone else on social media. Taking the time to actually travel through the real world that we may pass by thoughtlessly every day will help us to empathise with one another, to help one another, and to reconstruct that real sense of community that our villages, towns and cities once possessed.

We can't all live like Jesus. We all have our complicated lives, our messy situations – and Jesus isn't asking us all to imitate Him literally in every sense. What He does want us to imitate, though, are His loving heart, His open eyes, His healing hands and His dusty feet. If we as Christians are to embrace, love, heal the world, we are going to have to live in it – properly, fully immersed. It is no good passing over it in our polluting planes far above the needs of the poor beneath us – or zooming past it on a motorway. We must learn, then, to use travel as a means of doing God's work, just as Jesus did, albeit in a modern context. After all, how are we to make disciples of all nations if we keep ourselves enclosed in our own metal boxes, zooming straight past at seventy miles per hour? This is little better than staying at home and not going out into the world at all. If we are to attract others to our life-changing faith, we need to be proactive about interacting with them. We need to make a point of travelling gently, in a way that everyone can see, so as to demonstrate our love for God's planet and His people.

The key point with travel, then, is this: travel privately as little as you can, and publically as much as you can. Private cars are inefficient, polluting, shut us off from the world and in many cases turn us into angry, frustrated motorists. Some people depend upon them through genuine need – such as having a disability or living in a very remote location, and they do have their uses for most of us from time to time. Some places are simply inaccessible except by car. But it is good to do as much local travel as we can on foot, leaving more time and meeting more people. It is better for health and for the planet, and for our Christian mission. Walk or cycle to church, to school, to work – and if possible move your home or your workplace to make this feasible. This will not be a possibility for everyone, but the more who do this, the less traffic there will be, and the better our local environment and the safety of the roads will be for everyone. This in turn will allow more people to travel slowly, and to meet others along the way. It will also be very beneficial in terms of greenhouse gas emissions.

This is not a new idea, but an ancient one: nobody would have considered plying their trade miles from where they lived before the twentieth-century explosion of motorcar use, which has turned too many places into dangerous, smelly and ugly networks of roads that blight God's Earth. As you walk, enjoy coming to know and love your local environment, and the neighbours you share it with.

Walking is a form of public travel, but it will not do for all journeys. In centuries past, horses were needed to go further afield, and we still have the descendants of horse-drawn stagecoaches: buses and trains. Whilst still potentially polluting, these vehicles are much more efficient than private cars because they carry so many people on the same journey, and they can of course be fantastic places to interact positively with others precisely because they are shared. Would Jesus today have ridden the bus? I think probably yes, and He would have met many needy people in doing so.

Whether a smile or a 'thank you', or a lengthier conversation if circumstances allow, public transport provides ample opportunity to enjoy relationships with other people whom we might not otherwise meet. These relationships – not the places we are always so desperate to get to or the things we might achieve when we get there – are what life is really all about. Try sharing a greeting when on a bus or train, and see what joy it can generate within you.

Trains can also take you a surprisingly long way; I for one once travelled from Singapore to London by train, a journey that took sixteen days with many stops, but which brought much more fulfilment than a sixteen hour flight might provide. Over land, one can truly interact with cultures and experience other peoples, appreciating more fully the vastness of the Earth – and its fragility. Not all long-distance journeys over land take this long, and if we do find ourselves travelling from far afield, is there really such a great rush to get home, that we cannot take a few days to do it? Is there really such a desperate need to get to some far away holiday destination, that we cannot take the time to go slowly and sustainably, and appreciate all that we see on the way? Or else, not to go so far at all, but to cherish a shorter journey, on foot or public transport, through places and amongst people that we have failed to appreciate nearer to home?

Christians, then, are called to travel. The Gospels give many examples of this. But we are not all called to travel great distances on a regular basis, and are not called to use polluting aeroplanes. We are called to travel in a way that emulates Jesus, that shows reverence for God's beautiful creation and delights in its inhabitants. We are not to allow this fast-paced modern world to distract us or lead us astray, to tell us that we always need to go as fast as we can, or to tick off all the famous sights across the world in order to obtain fulfilment in life. Our fulfilment comes through Jesus, not through to-do lists. Furthermore, if we race around in order to fill each moment with productivity, we shall soon find that our lives are in fact empty and impoverished; and if we carelessly over-use polluting forms of transport, we shall destroy the very world we wanted to see and appreciate.

Jesus calls us, then, to abandon the baggage of the modern-day quest for 'success', and to travel light, with our hearts open to God and our eyes open to His world. It is a Christian duty to refrain from flying, at least for now, as much as possible – because we know what damage aeroplanes do to the creation we are charged to look after. It is a Christian duty to travel amongst God's people, not above them, and to get our feet dirty trampling the byways and interacting with real, living communities and individuals around us. It is a Christian duty to leave the polluting car behind wherever practicable, to sacrifice convenience for the sake of experience and to prioritise the life of the world over the short-term gains of fast travel. If we walk or cycle wherever possible, we can begin to live out a Christian duty to care for creation and our own communities. Travel slowly, travel light, and greet those whom you meet along the way, for the time has come to share Christ's message with the whole world. And travel humbly, as lambs among wolves – for it is God who will show us the safe way to go.

6

Blessed are the Poor

> Blessed be ye poor, for yours is the kingdom of God. (Luke 6:20)

In Luke chapter 6, we learn of Jesus' 'sermon on the plain', the equivalent of the 'sermon on the mount' in Matthew's Gospel. The location of the sermon is immaterial; what is important is the radical teaching that it contains. In the particular famous phrase quoted above, the beginning of the 'Beatitudes', Jesus turns the wisdom of the world on its head. It is not the rich who are blessed, with their many possessions, as would have been assumed. Rather, it is the poor who are blessed (happy), because though they have very little in material terms they possess the single most important thing of all: the Kingdom of God.

Unlike many of the issues we have already encountered in this book, which raise ethical objections primarily because of the environmental crisis of today – food, clothing, transport – having many possessions already posed serious ethical and religious questions in Jesus' own time, and surfeit goods are therefore subject to quite extensive explicit teaching in the Gospels. For Jesus' contemporaries, there was very little choice over what to eat; bread and fish were staples of the diet and hard to live without, and there was no such thing as factory farming, nor were methane emissions or overfishing issues at all. Only the very rich could be criticised for banqueting lavishly whilst the poor starved, as in the story of Lazarus the beggar (Luke 16). Fine clothing was rare, and few of Jesus' listeners could afford it, nor did it pose serious environmental risks. Travel was simple and not polluting at all. But gathering many possessions was – then as much as now – a temptation with the power to do great harm.

Yes, most of Jesus' followers were poor, and likely had few possessions. However, in their time as much as in our own, possessions and riches were an aspiration in the eyes of many – worldly wisdom taught that having many possessions and much wealth was the mark of a successful life. It is this erroneous assumption that Jesus says so much to counter in the Gospels. Indeed, by His own life of poverty He explicitly demonstrates His opposition to such a fallacy.

Possessions did not, at that time, carry the environmental consequences that they bring with them today. Nowadays, by 'possessions' we often mean all the gadgets, trinkets and 'clutter' sold to us in massive quantities, much of it made of plastic and requiring vastly more energy and resources to make and transport than seems justified, considering how little importance is given to any individual item in our full houses. Much of it we do not really need, or even really want. First-century people possessed few of these sorts of surplus things. Rather, by 'possessions' in its Biblical use we can read lands and tenants as much as we can material objects. The rich would own much land and reap the profits of its cultivation – their lands were 'possessions' that they did not really need, but which brought with them coveted riches and respect.

The main point for Jesus is not actually what the possessions are – more important is the fact that, whatever they are, they come to possess us. Indeed, I do not think that we should interpret Jesus as condemning all forms of ownership in the Gospels – just as 'your Father knoweth that you need' food and clothing, He knows that we need houses, land and some material goods. What Jesus condemns, though, is our setting our hearts upon these things, gathering goods to ourselves as if that was the very purpose of life, rather than using them to serve God and help each other. A clue to this comes from Matthew's wording of the Beatitude with which this chapter opened: 'blessed are the poor in spirit' (Matthew 5:3). It is left to the reader to interpret what is meant by 'poor in spirit', but it likely means those who, regardless of how much wealth they have, are not possessed by that wealth, but are free to use it or lose it or give it away without resentment. They continue to be humble, regarding the poor as equals and giving to others.

Another of Jesus' parables makes a similar point. In Luke 12 we read of a 'certain rich man' who had a lot of land, which brought forth a lot of produce. There was nothing wrong with this – indeed, many might think that this man had been blest in his good fortune by God. The problem lay with how the rich man responded to this blessing. Having too much produce, he refused to give some of it to those in need and to share it with others. Instead, he built bigger barns in order to store it up for himself. No sooner had he done this, than the rich man died – and all this wealth was suddenly worthless to him. It did not help him when he was alive, since all he did was store it up, and nor did he allow it to help others whom it might have benefited. All this excess did not help him to stave off death, even for a moment. Had he shared it with others whilst he lived, he might have created much love, joy and friendship. Instead, it is implied that he will face judgement for misusing what has been given him. Riches and excess of wealth, which could have enabled this man to do enormous good, have corrupted him, and even endangered his soul. He has been undone by his own possessions. 'So is he that layeth up treasure for himself,' Jesus goes on, 'and is not rich towards God.'

This parable was spoken in response to two brothers squabbling about inheritance. They asked Jesus to intervene in the dispute, as though the inheritance of wealth was important enough for Him to arbitrate over. For Jesus, though, riches are not what is important in life – and indeed distract us from what is truly important. Life is about so much more than material wealth – it's about wealth of relationships and wealth of love, wherein is found true joy. 'Take heed and beware of covetousness,' He warns them, 'for a man's life consisteth not in the abundance of the things which he possesseth.' The message could not be clearer.

Jesus expanded upon the point of riches not being important, or even a hindrance in life, in many other parables. There is the parable of the unjust steward in Luke 16, in which the steward is commended for using the 'mammon of unrighteousness' to make himself friends. Knowing that he is about to be dismissed, he writes off debts owed to his master, essentially giving to the poor, to win the greater gift of friendship. He is even commended by his master for doing so. Whilst some find it puzzling that Jesus seems to be encouraging dishonesty here, what He is really commending is the fact that the 'unjust steward' is using whatever power he still has to help others – and, importantly, is using his power to forgive others, even though really their debts are owed to his master, not to him. Likewise, everything that we have rightly belongs to God, and we all owe debts to Him because of our sins and our failure to use rightly what he has given us. Yet that should never stop us sharing God's wealth with others – wealth is there to be shared, not hoarded – or forgiving our neighbours.

Then there is the poor woman who, in lovingly putting into the Temple collection a mite – all that she can afford – to help others in need, gives more than the rich who cast in out of their abundance of riches, as recorded in Luke 21. There is also the famous 'certain ruler' of Luke 18, who asks Jesus, 'what must I do to inherit eternal life?' – in other words, how do I obtain the Kingdom of Heaven? Jesus is pleased that the man has kept the Ten Commandments, but He asks of him one thing more: 'sell all that thou hast, and distribute unto the poor, and thou shalt have treasure in heaven: and come, follow me.' When the ruler heard this, we are told that he was sorrowful, because he was very rich. Evidently, he treasured his riches more than he treasured following Jesus, loath to give them up even in exchange for eternal life. The deceitfulness of riches is powerful indeed.

Does Jesus, then, demand that we sell everything that we have and give the money to the poor? Not necessarily. Clearly, not everyone can sell all they own, or else there would be nobody to buy it, and life would become impossible if nobody had homes or food or clothes or the tools with which to do their work and make these essentials for others. Nor are Christians intended to be a small, peculiar people who renounce all these things and depend upon the charity of everyone else. St Paul famously continued to work as a tentmaker to earn a living whilst preaching the Gospel – and would need to possess the tools of his trade. What is significant about this story is that Jesus knows that this man's particular vice is his attachment to material possessions, and that is why Jesus instructs this particular man as He does. Break the attachment, and the man will be free to follow Jesus. Yet those who own material things – even sometimes those that are rich – do not always share this vice. After all, despite going on to say that it is easier for a camel to pass through the eye of a needle than for a rich man to enter God's Kingdom, Jesus says that this is in fact possible – 'the things that are impossible with men are possible with God.'

It is, then, possible for a rich man to love God more than his riches, and to use those riches to help others and to serve God – and it must thus be possible for all of us to use whatever wealth we have to the same end. The difficulty is that money and wealth are both corrupting and deceptive: the richer you are, the more difficult it is not to be possessed by your riches, and the harder it is to give a large proportion of your wealth to others. The very existence of billionaires proves this.

All of this gains a new impetus in our modern age of environmental crisis, because the material possessions we buy – whether to keep or to throw away – nowadays have a considerable impact on the lives of others. The capitalist commercialism that has arisen especially during the second half of the twentieth century encourages excess consumption of material goods and the resources required to produce them, and is in no way compatible with the way of life espoused in the Gospels. Our houses today are filled with so much more material plenty than those of any of our ancestors, much of which we do not use or need. Consumer gadgets that claim to make life easier clutter our kitchens and living rooms; children are encouraged to play with voluminous quantities of plastic toys; and nearly every adult has a car. All of this requires vast amounts of metal, crude oil and other polluting materials to produce, and whilst recycling rates are improving much of it still ends up dumped in the ground, leeching toxic chemicals into the waterways, or burnt in a third-world country where the fumes choke the lungs of the poorest.

These things cause real harm to other people and to God's world – aside from the electricity or fuel needed to power them – and yet we are always encouraged to buy more and more of them, to upgrade to the latest 'phone, to get a new car after just two or three years, to replace one polyester sofa with a newer, more fashionable one, to help the economy grow – as if that was the purpose of life. But these things do not in their abundance improve our lives: they clutter our lives, possess our lives, demanding our attention and refusing to let us be at peace. Often, we are bombarded with adverts for new things even as we are using the old ones, always being commanded and cajoled to buy something else. Jesus often went up the mountain to pray, taking nothing with Him. The polyphony of gadgets of the modern age makes it impossible to escape and to do what we are really made to do – to enjoy a relationship with God and with other beings free from the distractions of covetousness.

This is not to say that these modern technologies do not have their uses, or that we should do without them altogether. Many have the potential to bring great joy into our own and others' lives if used correctly – to connect us with family and friends who are far away or to help us express our creativity. Again, just as in Jesus' time, it is not the material goods themselves that are the problem – it is whether they possess us and distract us from God and His purposes. When it comes to material possessions, then, simplicity is the important thing. As Christians, we know that these things are not an ends in themselves: they are a means to live this life, and the real ends come at the end of life – the reward of the Kingdom of Heaven.

We should seek, then, not to have many possessions, but only enough possessions to make the most out of life. We are called to enter a kind of poverty – a voluntary poverty, one of going without excess, rather than the much more negative spectre of involuntary poverty that blights the lives of so many in our unequal world. The latter is a poverty in which people go without their basic needs, and is in many ways caused by a lack of the former – by the over-consumption of the richest and a failure to share the Earth's resources fairly. It is by embracing a voluntary poverty, then, that we can truly help others in need, that we can become 'poor in spirit', and that our lives can be enriched.

We must refuse to upgrade to the latest version of a 'phone or computer or whatever when the old one is working just fine. Some of us can live without a 'phone or a computer, or both entirely – and if this is possible we should do it, for any unnecessary possession is a stumbling block that holds us back from following Jesus. If we do need these things, we should get them second-hand where possible, or made from recycled materials, or share them with others so that fewer devices are needed overall. The same, really, goes for everything we possess. We must not allow any material thing to possess us – otherwise it becomes an idol. For many, the smartphone has become the idol of the modern world, as it comes to take over nearly every aspect of life. It comes at a huge environmental cost – many precious metals are needed to produce it – and becomes an all-consuming distraction from the real world. This must be resisted, and if it starts to enslave us, it should be dispensed with altogether. Though the smartphone may be appropriate for some professions, it has become far, far to ubiquitous, foisted upon everyone because it makes money for big corporations selling the 'phone itself or the data that can be harvested from it. We must not allow this to happen, especially at the expense of our beautiful planet. Indeed, we must not hearken to any marketing ploy to make us buy for the sake of buying – for it leads us away from the true meaning of life.

If we all live more simply, the saying goes, others will be able to simply live. Minimising how much stuff we replace – at home or in church – helps us to keep our lives clearer for God, but also helps to reduce the massive environmental costs of feeding lifestyles of consumption. There are many ways in which we can shop sustainably – look for paper packaging and not plastic, choose reusable over disposable (and actually reuse it!), buy wooden toys for children and let them play with simpler things, or explore the outdoors more. We can also buy energy-efficient appliances when we need to. But better is always to re-use what we have, rather than to replace; to repair rather than to throw away; and to buy second-hand rather than new. We will all always need things and should follow guidelines such as these when we get them. Better by far is not to buy at all, however, from the perspective of the environment, and to make do with little – treasuring only that which we need to live a fulfilling life. Jesus teaches us that we should give whatever else we have away, or the money that we save in not buying more things. In this way, we not only help our environment and our needy neighbour; dispossessed of the demon of material excess, we also set free our own souls, and trade in our trinkets for the Kingdom of God.

7

Discerning the Time

> When ye see a cloud rise out of the west, straightway ye say, 'There cometh a shower'; and so it is. Ye hypocrites, ye can discern the face of the sky and of the earth; but how is it that ye do not discern this time? (Luke 12:54-55)

Since time immemorial, humans have been using the sky to predict the weather. Over the past one hundred and fifty years or so, scientists have been able to produce increasingly sophisticated forecasts, so that with the aid of modern supercomputers we can predict the weather for days ahead. Scientists use those same computer models to trace longer-term changes in the average weather conditions – what we might call a 'climate forecast' as opposed to a weather forecast. When the models predict that a storm is coming, by and large people listen. They take an umbrella, they cancel or move indoors the garden party, they drive rather than walk to work. The weather forecast goes out at prime time on the radio and television.

Yet when these models predict that the Earth will increase in temperature by 4 degrees Celsius by the end of the century, that thousands of species will become extinct, that parts of the world will become uninhabitable and that life will be made much harder for everyone, and that it's all because of human emissions of carbon dioxide and methane, often they don't listen. First, they deny – human-made climate change was an established fact by 1990, yet 'climate denial' was still common twenty-five years later. Then, seeing the signs of changing weather patterns, they reluctantly accept that it's happening. Yet they don't stop flying, or eating meat, or driving petrol cars beyond necessity, or buying new giant televisions. They know the consequences of these actions, but they won't stop doing them. 'Ye hypocrites', Jesus says to us all. 'Ye can discern the face of the sky and of the earth; but how is it that ye do not discern this time?'

When Jesus speaks these words, He is referring to a very special time: the time of His coming, the time when God is among His people in human form. He is criticising the people of that time for not recognising His significance, though they can recognise the significance of the signs in the sky regarding what the weather will be like. Yet His words, as so often, are also applicable to our own time – painfully applicable in this case. We see the signs, we know what to do to avert disaster, and yet we do not do it.

This is the case for humanity as a whole – or at least for that portion of humanity that have the power to act, because the poorest in the world have little impact on climate change and little choice in how they live in any case. Sadly, it is also the case for the Christian Church. The Church seems not to have taken environmental concerns seriously at all over recent decades, instead focussing its attention on other issues – issues which may well be very important, such as helping the needy in our own neighbourhoods, but which must not deafen us to Christ's call on us to care for the wider world, and its people, whom our actions and lifestyles are putting in danger.

Environmental injustice is the greatest injustice of our time – greater still than the myriad other injustices that confront us in the modern world. A few pollute very much, and many suffer very much as a result. We as Christians must not be perpetrators of this injustice, any more than we would want to be part of any other form of injustice in the world, such as those surrounding race, gender and sexuality. Jesus' words call us to perceive the time we are living in, a time of great inequality where Earth is ravaged by greed. They call on us to respond to this time with love and with the too often neglected virtue of humility, and to recognise the duty that we all have to act.

Climate change, disastrous as it may be in and of itself, is to us primarily a sign. It is a symbol of the abominable state of human society today, a society that allows the global poor to slave away mining resources and manufacturing surplus goods for the rich, or to starve in countries ruined by changed weather patterns while the richest continue to over-consume and throw away copious quantities of waste. The profit-driven system of today's global economy, whereby rich corporations strip nature's resources in order to sell things that people do not really need, using clever marketing tricks to do so, is not Christian. It is exploitative of the environment, of the Earth's inhabitants, of workers and of those who buy the products. Any system that relies on people buying as much as possible regardless of real need cannot be environmentally sustainable. And tinkering with products to make them slightly more energy-efficient or recyclable does little to address this fundamental issue. It does not solve the problem of simply making too much stuff, eating too much meat, and travelling too quickly too often.

Christ calls us to simplicity, so that we might focus on a loving God and on each other. Doing so requires us to escape from this consumerist cycle and take responsibility for the consequences of our everyday choices in what is, from a global perspective, a wealthy society. There is much done nowadays to address the racial aspect of colonialism – though even in this regard efforts continue to fall short. For the most part, however, colonialism always was and still is primarily about economic exploitation: the richer nations of the world exploiting and enslaving the poorer ones. In this sense, colonialism is still alive and well: in the sweatshops producing cheap clothes in Asia for people to wear and throw away in Europe and North America; in the mines of China and Africa extracting minerals to make mobile 'phones and car batteries for use in the West – colonialism, with working conditions little better than slavery, carries on. Oil is a big factor too, as western oil companies scour the globe to find and extract new deposits – even in our current climate-conscious age – heedless of the local and global consequences.

In spite of a lot of words being bandied about, these things still go on, they still make money for the big corporations, and they still make misery for the poorest. The countries being exploited may have independence, yet they are often riddled with internal corruption and external interference. In any case, the skin colour of those in charge makes little difference: wherever nature and culture is being ripped up to feed the greed of the richest, colonialism carries on. To support such a system is not Christian.

There are some even today within the Christian Church who claim that climate change, biodiversity loss and the state of the environment are not something that we should worry about. Leave it to God, they say, and all will be fine. He created the Earth for us to use, and the end of the world is coming soon anyway. Nothing could be further than this from the attitude lived out and taught by Jesus, as we have seen throughout the chapters of this book. When God created us, He created us to be stewards of His creation, to look after it and not to destroy it. He intended us to have loving relationships with Him and with one another, not to exploit each other and create needless suffering.

We want to live in a pleasant, habitable, healthy environment, regardless of how long it will be until the end times, and Christ shows us that it is our duty, and must become our joy, to care for the needy in our midst. We must remember that we are not passive players in the environmental crisis. If we as individuals and as a Church continue to make regular flights, to buy more and more consumer goods that we do not need, to eat industrially produced meat and to conform to fast fashion, we are by those very actions causing harm to the poorest and most needy in the world. We are creating the storms that destroy harvests and devastate communities. We are driving the modern-day slavery of precious metal mines and the contamination of vital water supplies with the associated filth. We are causing rainforest to be cut down and communities that rely upon it to be devastated. We are making animals live lives of suffering and pain, and we are destroying species that God has lovingly made, many of which we depend on for our own survival through services such as pollination that they provide. None of this is in any way compatible with loving God or loving our neighbours as ourselves. It is time that we recognised this, and our moral obligation to live more sustainable lives.

The aim of this short book has been to show a few ways in which we can do this, together, as Christians. In a sense, the environmental issue is one that has crept up on us, and we have only recently come to recognise our own moral duty in this matter. It is not an issue that our forebears, by-and-large, had to consider, for it is only in the past few decades that consumerism has seen an explosion of consumption per capita in the western world and the associated environmental harms. It has become normal in our culture to eat industrialised meat every day (think of all the fast food chains that have sprung up to facilitate this) – but it is our Christian duty not to do so. It has become normal to fly away on holiday at least once a year – it is our Christian duty to resist this temptation. It has become normal to treat clothes as disposable, rather than to 'make do and mend', and to have 'smartphones' in every pocket and huge televisions in every house. It is our Christian duty, not necessarily to avoid such technologies completely, but to be considerate about what we really need, and the harms that getting more than this might bring, and to buy as little new as possible. To make do with what we already have, and to buy second-hand or to seek to repair rather than to replace with new is an act of Christian compassion.

Ultimately, if we pray to God for a healthy planet, and for the aversion of disasters like storms and floods and heat-waves, we must pray in our actions as well as in our words. We must seek to live sustainably if we want to see a sustainable world – that is, one in which human civilisation and life as a whole can continue to flourish indefinitely. We must show the world that there is a much better way, drawing our fulfilment in life from God and from one another rather than from money and abundance of material things. It is our Christian calling to evangelise for this way of life by living it ourselves.

Can we really be a Church that cares, a Church that follows Christ, and still be using plastic 'disposable' cups and serving processed ham sandwiches, cutting the churchyard grass down to within an inch of its life, spraying weed-killer and jetting off regularly on our holidays? I do not believe that we can. Not all of us can do all that is required for a sustainable society on our own or all the time – at least, not from the starting point we are currently in. It takes time and effort to change the status quo, the form new habits, to go against the grain of current normality. The gas-fired boiler we need for warmth and the petrol car we have to drive to access amenities may be beyond our means to replace or avoid. Yet there are small things we can all do, day by day, to make the world a better place – whether it is taking the train rather than a plane, going vegetarian every other day or leaving our grass uncut for 'no mow May'. God sees all these small sacrifices; He sees the fact that we care – and so will many of our neighbours.

The important thing is that we consciously do all that we can do to show love towards our planet and its many and varied inhabitants, by making those choices that we know will make a difference for good. We cannot get everything right all of the time, or sacrifice everything that we have – and God isn't asking us to. But whatever we can do is a prayer in and of itself, a small action perhaps but an action of humility and love. And God will gather up and treasure those little acts of love, and He will magnify them, and together we will make a real difference to our planet and the lives of the people upon it.

At the end of Matthew's Gospel, Jesus assures us, 'I am with you always, even unto the end of the age.' Let us let Him be with us and in us, guiding us in humble lives of simple trust and simple needs, towards a better tomorrow for everyone.

www.ingramcontent.com/pod-product-compliance
Lightning Source LLC
Chambersburg PA
CBHW052151070526
44585CB00017B/2063